MY DIARY
1979

PAMELA JAYNE

ILLUSTRATED BY
ELIZABETH BAKER-BARTLETT

Matador
9 Priory Business Park,
Wistow Road, Kibworth Beauchamp,
Leicestershire. LE8 0RX
Tel: 0116 279 2299
Email: books@troubador.co.uk
Web: www.troubador.co.uk/matador
Twitter: @matadorbooks

ISBN 978 1789015 935

British Library Cataloguing in Publication Data.
A catalogue record for this book is available from the British Library.

Printed and bound in the UK by T J International, Padstow, Cornwall
Typeset in 11pt Adobe Garamond Pro by Troubador Publishing Ltd, Leicester, UK

Matador is an imprint of Troubador Publishing Ltd

Proceeds from the sales of this book will be donated to The Wallich, a charity which offers accommodation and support services to some of the most vulnerable and marginalised people in Wales to enable them to live happier, safer and more independent lives.

To Pamela,

Merry Christmas 1978

love from Hazel

and Kevin.

Contents

Monday 25th December 1978

Lovely day. Had sports bag, cords, top, this diary, pen, a new toothbrush, toothpaste, brush & comb set, 2 pairs pants, 2 pairs socks and a game. Watched the Sound of Music on TV. It was very good but was better when we saw it in colour at the Scala. Wuthering Heights, Matchstick Men and Summer Nights were on Christmas Top of the Pops. Mary's Boy Child by Boney M is number one. Mike Yarwood's Christmas Special was funny.

Tuesday 26th December 1978

Went over Grandad & Grama's in Trelewis as usual on Boxing Day. Had leek soup, turkey and trifle. It is a mystery what Grama puts into her trifle, it is a mix up of things but always very tasty. Lost a part of my new game. I wish I could find it.

Wednesday 27th December 1978

Dad went to market and Grandad Jack stayed in bed. Looked for the bit for my game again. Watched All Star Record Breakers with Roy Castle. The Blue Peter gang were on it. Simon Groom, Peter Purvis, John Noakes and Lesley Judd. They were all dressed up in old fashioned music hall clothes, singing and dancing. Very disappointing.

Thursday 28th December 1978

Helped dad bed down the cows over the barn. The barn is always warm when the cows are in, they are like radiators. Me, Susan and Greg made food out of plasticine and played cafes all afternoon. Watched Blue Peter Review of the Year. Abba was on it.

Friday 29th December 1978

The telephone man came and fixed our telephone today. Our telephone number used to be 295 but now it has 4 numbers. Watched Citizen Smith this evening. Wolfie is my favourite.

Saturday 30th December 1978

Aunty Lynne came down from England and fetched her hairdryer. It was very good. I would love to have one. Susan and I are babysitting Laurence tonight. Aunty Ann and Uncle Jeff are going out. It is snowing.

Sunday 31st December 1978

Aunty Ann and Uncle Jeff came back early as it was so cold. They had to leave their car in Penrhiw in Brynithel and walk back. It was like a blizzard. Uncle Jeff had icicles hanging from his eyebrows.

Monday 1 January 1979

Started typing a book on my typewriter. Don't know when I'll finish it, hopefully before school starts next week. Uncle Jeff's car is still stuck in the snow down Penrhiw.

Tuesday 2 January 1979

Did lots more typing. Sid Vicious the punk was on the News. His band is called the Sex Pistols, I don't know how he gets away with it. And now he has murdered his girlfriend.

Wednesday 3 January 1979

The first chapter of my book is finished. I have named it The Den and designed the cover. Snowing again.

Thursday 4 January 1979

Got the Lego out today and made a bungalow. Watched Top of the Pops. Village People are number 1 with YMCA.

Friday 5 January 1979

Went shopping with mam, looking for a hacking jacket. Then went for my piano lesson. My piano teacher is Mrs Lane who lives by Debbie Tibbs and who is Sharon Tingle's nan. She charges 50p. Shaun Doughnut Martin is having lessons too but is not very good. His legs are so short he can't reach the pedals.

Saturday 6 January 1979

Helped dad feed the sheep. Nigel Creed and Mark Peat came to call for me and we went sleighing down the field on sacks.

Sunday 7 January 1979

There is a strike. Lorry drivers. The News says food might not be able to get to the shops. I am excited to get back to school tomorrow. I miss my friends. Watched a good film about a horse.

Monday 8 January 1979

School was good. Ann Davies, Keri Gould, Keri Bevan and I are practising for a concert to put on down the steps in the school yard. The flat bit is our stage and the steps are seats for the audience. We have learned all the words to YMCA and Ann is writing out the words to A Little More Love by Oliver Newton John.

Tuesday 9 January 1979

Fights in the school yard today. Our gang against another. They wouldn't let us practise our concert. So Mrs Sellick the dinner lady has banned all concerts.

Wednesday 10 January 1979

Horrible day in school. It was snowing so we had to stay in the classroom all day and the electric went out. Mr Courtney the caretaker was walking around looking glum as usual.

Thursday 11 January 1979

Have had enough of dinner lady Mrs Sellick. First she bans our concert and then she puts salt on our ice slide and sends us over the boys' yard.

Friday 12 January 1979

I have decided to get my Speaker badge in Girl Guides. I have chosen to talk about the potato. I have to talk about it for 5 minutes. I can already name some different types and different ways of cooking them.

Saturday 13 January 1979

Greg had his 5th birthday party today. The Bowds (Janine, Samantha and Andrew) came. Laurence couldn't because he was bad. Played Pass the Parcel, Musical Chairs and Musical Statues.

Sunday 14 January 1979

While putting felt pens away in chocolate tin, it reminded me of Christmas and then I had a terrible thought, Christmas is all over.

Monday 15 January 1979

Greg's birthday. Cut my hand on a piece of glass doing a cartwheel in the school yard. Keri G and I went down the infants to help give out the milk. John Craven's Newsround says people are panicking about food running out because there are no lorries to fetch it to the shops. I hope the strike ends soon.

Tuesday 16 January 1979

The glass is still in my hand. Our teacher Mr Parfitt put ointment on it. Mrs Bray used to be the one we went to for things like that. She pulled my tooth out once. I used to like watching her pulling people's teeth out at the front of the class.

Wednesday 17 January 1979

Came home from school at dinner time because of the snow. Watched Ludwig, a strange alien egg thing that saves animals and plays Beethoven music. Hope I'll be able to go back to school tomorrow.

Thursday 18 January 1979

Couldn't go back to school because it's still snowing. Worrying about not being able to go to the Guides disco on Saturday. I will ring Ann to see what it's like down Brynithel.

Friday 19 January 1979

Mam went shopping to Abertillery and came back like a snowman.

Saturday 20 January 1979

Mam has brought two of our mountain ponies down to the shed to break in for me and Susan. I have named mine Farrah after Farrah Fawcett Majors from Charlies Angels because of her big mane. She is a skewbald. Susan's is all brown and she is calling her Bunty after her favourite comic. Guides disco has been cancelled.

Sunday 21 January 1979

Started reading Enid Blyton's Book of Brownies to Greg. Mam let Farrah and Bunty out of the shed. They are a bit wild and scary.

Monday 22 January 1979

No school again today, not because of the snow this time but because of another strike. John Craven says it's a big one. There are no cooks or lollypop ladies working today. Mrs Kimber will be able to put her feet up.

Tuesday 23 January 1979

Still the snow is bad. No school again. Hope we have a good summer after this. I feel sorry for the sheep and its hard work for dad.

Wednesday 24 January 1979

Getting fed up now. Can't do anything except play lego in this weather. Ended up watching Pebble Mill and Touché Turtle. Will try going outside tomorrow.

Thursday 25 January 1979

Susan is very stubborn. She won't join in the Puss in Boots play I have written and Greg is upset because he was looking forward to it. Got dressed up warm to walk over Aunty Ann's but ended up in trouble for tramping snow everywhere.

Friday 26 January 1979

Mam had to go shopping in the snow again. I checked on Farrah and then stayed in with my book, the Folk of the Faraway Tree. It was a peaceful afternoon.

Saturday 27 January 1979

Swap Shop was good. Wanted to make a swap but didn't have anything to swap with. Looked through Kays catalogue instead and chose who I would have as my husband and the furniture I would have in my house.

Sunday 28 January 1979

I want to go to school tomorrow but the snow is still too bad. Had a row with mam this evening over having a bath. The bathroom is freezing and if we're not going to school what's the point. Listened to the Top 40 on Radio 1. Ian Dury and the Blockheads are number one with Hit Me With Your Rhythm Stick.

Monday 29 January 1979

Had a fright today. Dad had to take cattle to market. We took an hour coming down the hill in the landrover with the cattle box behind us. We kept sliding on the snow and the ice. The box went sideways. It was very scary.

Tuesday 30 January 1979

Finally went back to school today. Had a lift in Raquel's car. She is very annoying. Maria is getting her hair crimped. Andrew from the third year got a lump on his head from Mr Bevan's blackboard rubber.

Wednesday 31 January 1979

Made an excuse that I had to meet someone so I didn't have to go in Raquel's car again. Maria came to school like a model with her crimped hair, burgundy jumper dress and adidas sports bag.

Thursday 1 February 1979

Lots of birthdays this month. Ann Davies (11), Owen Price (11), my cousin Kirsten Paulson (5) who lives in America, Leanda Combstock (3) who lives over the lane and Grandad Jack (70) who lives in the front room.

Friday 2 February 1979

Went to piano lessons then Guides and did my speech about the potato. I will get my Speaker badge now. Our teacher Mr Parfitt has entered our school, Ty'r Graig, into a gymnastic competition. Very excited about that.

Saturday 3 February 1979

I am going to try and get more Guides badges. I think I could get Toymaker, First Aider, Cyclist, Gardener, Dancer, Crafter and Writer. Bell Ringer and Braille Reader maybe not. Sid Vicious the punk died.

Sunday 4 February 1979

Dad is going to buy a new muck spreader and Greg is excited. Farrah and Bunty are starting to calm down, they let us quite near them today. Listened to the Top 40 charts. Blondie is number 1 with Heart of Glass.

Monday 5 February 1979

Today our school minibus driver Rose was late so she drove us right into the schoolyard, it was terrible. I thought she was going to run over Doughnut and Youngy who were playing football.

Tuesday 6 February 1979

Me and Ann are going to get our hair cut at the House of Curls. Awful wind this evening. Kept me awake.

Wednesday 7 February 1979

Was nearly sick in school. Wednesday dinners, always the same. Mashed potatoes with yellow lumps, soggy cabbage, swampy gravy and for afters custard with skin. Our school cook is named Gloria and she is Linda Russell's mam. She is very nice but I feel sorry for Linda having to eat food like that all the time.

Thursday 8 February 1979

Stayed behind for netball with Miss Gill. The boys made valentine cards. Horrible ones. Mine said Roses are red, violets are blue, cabbage is green and so are you. Shaun Doughnut Martin, Robert Jazzy Jarrett, Martin Crockett and Gareth Larcombe. They think they are funny but they are not.

Friday 9 February 1979

Snowed again last night. We had to sit in the television room with the younger kids this morning and watch Look and Read with the irritating Wordy. Quarrelled with Ann so went in Mr Reed's class at breaktime. The toughest girl in our year was in there, Gail Hayes.

Saturday 10 February 1979

Snow drifts 10-foot-high when I woke up this morning. Some of our sheep could be buried. It is a worrying time.

Sunday 11 February 1979

Not feeling well. Farrah let us stroke her at last but Bunty is still playing up. Listened to the Top 40 charts on Radio 1.

Monday 12 February 1979

Snow. No school. Grandad Jack's 70th birthday. Still not feeling well. Susan is behaving terrible. She is as stubborn as her horse.

Tuesday 13 February 1979

Snow. No school. Mrs Williams from Castle Cottage has had a heart attack and Grandad Jack is having trouble breathing. The road is still blocked with snow so dad had to carry a tank of oxygen up the hill on his back.

Wednesday 14 February 1979

Snow. No school. Listened to K-Tel Action Replay on the record player. Rat Trap, Hanging on the Telephone, Toast, Stumbling in and I Lost my Heart to a Starship Trooper. Taught Greg how to do the Boney M Rasputin dance.

Thursday 15 February 1979

Snow. No school. Ann Davies' birthday. Started making a rag doll for the Girl Guide Toymaker badge. Susan is making one too, she is good for her age. Hope we'll be able to go back to school soon.

Friday 16 February 1979

Snow. No school. Susan and I sorted our bedroom. Wanted to throw out my patch pockets because they are now old fashioned but mam said to keep them as playing clothes. Watched Superstars this evening. Brian Jacks the judo champion won.

Saturday 17 February 1979

Susan and I played wrestling and then fashion with the cut-out wardrobes from the back page of her Bunty comics. Mam gave us Montego bars.

Sunday 18 February 1979

A phone call spoilt the day. I learnt that because of my absence at school we couldn't go in for the gymnastic competition. Also, that the Guides disco had happened on Saturday and so I have missed it. Made a cake.

Monday 19 February 1979

More snow. Even the Sahara Desert is getting snow. No school. Nigel Creed and Peatsy came to call for me so we could do more sliding down the field on sacks.

Tuesday 20 February 1979

Finally going back to school tomorrow. Went to Diane's hairdressers and got my hair cut, layered and winged. Watched Dallas this evening.

Wednesday 21 February 1979

Good news, the gymnastic competition was cancelled until the end of March so I haven't missed it and our school Ty'r Graig will be taking part.

Thursday 22 February 1979

Cut my head open practising gymnastics in the yard. Jumped into a handstand and my head landed first. Blood everywhere. Had to sit quietly in the television room with a bandage on my head. Susan was worried.

Friday 23 February 1979

Today the sun was shining. A lovely day at last. Me, Keri G and Ann helped our teacher Mr Parfitt. Watched Hong Kong Phooey before going to Guides. Had full marks in uniform inspection.

Saturday 24 February 1979

Watched the Dick Emery Show with Grandad Jack. It was funny. Mam didn't know, she was in the kitchen.

Sunday 25 February 1979

Earnt 25p by brasso-ing mam's brass ornaments. Got them sparkling. Taught Susan the Little Playmate clapping song. Watched a new programme, Wurzel Gummidge, a scarecrow that changes his head.

Monday 26 February 1979

Still sunny. Susan and I went to Abertillery gymnastics club. I am going to try and get some BAGA badges.

Tuesday 27 February 1979

Not so sunny today. Ann was in a mood and Dai Jones from the Carpenters Arms pub said he was going to fight me. He was out on his bike with his dog Micky after school so I stayed in and worked on my Toymaker badge. Watched Dallas.

Wednesday 28th February 1979

Ann fetched her Blue Jeans magazine to school and Maria fetched her Smash Hits. We learned the words to Tragedy by the Bee Gees.

Thursday 1 March 1979

St David's Day. The infants wore welsh costumes. Black hats, long skirts, pinnys and shawls for the girls and coal miners' clothes for the boys. Mam went shopping. Grandad Jack stayed in bed. Nurse came. Went to gymnastic club then watched Top of the Pops and Blankety Blank. Top of the Pops was good. The Cars with Just What I Needed, Skids with Into the Valley, Thin Lizzy with Waiting for an Alibi, Queen with Don't Stop me Now and Boney M with Painter Man. The Bees Gees are number 1 with Tragedy.

Friday 2 March 1979

Keri G and I were on tuck shop duty today. We made a good shop out of the gym benches in the hall. Chipmunk oxo crisps and KP beef burger Outer Spacers are in. Went to piano lessons, then Guides, then slept over Aunty Ann's house.

Saturday 3 March 1979

Babysat Laurence in morning then went shopping with Aunty Ann in afternoon. Had a nice time. Susan went with dad to check on the sheep and fetched a lamb back that we need to look after. We have named him JR after JR Ewing.

Sunday 4 March 1979

Dad is getting on my nerves. He says the Bee Gees are like singing mice and keeps laughing whenever Tragedy comes on the wireless. Started making a spaceship out of boxes for Greg.

Monday 5 March 1979

Finished making spaceship for Greg. He is not grateful. He says he's going to make a better one that he can fit Grandad Jack into and that will lift off the ground. Went to gymnastic club.

Tuesday 6 March 1979

Today Rose the Minibus ran over a dog outside the old people's complex with our minibus. We felt a bump and she said it was a stone but we looked out the window and saw her picking up a dog.

Wednesday 7 March 1979

In trouble with Miss Gill. Had to do 1000 lines. Had a spelling test and a tummy ache. Greg has made a big mess outside the front door where he is making his spaceship so he can tip Grandad Jack out of his chair into it.

Thursday 8 March 1979

Netball tournament next week. Got to stay behind on Monday to practice. Robert Young wants to be on the team. Doughnut said Youngy should have been named Nancy because he wants to be on the girls' netball team. So we are calling him Nancy from now on.

Friday 9 March 1979

Nancy practised netball with us but he is not good enough for the team. Went to piano lessons then Guides. We watched a film about America and had biscuits and Ribena.

Saturday 10 March 1979

Me, mam and Susan spent time with Farrah and Bunty today, to get them used to us. JR the lamb is certainly getting used to us, he is getting very cheeky.

Sunday 11 March 1979

Went to Nelson to visit Aunty Marg and Uncle Phil. Played with our cousin Jayne. She is good fun. We had spangles. Listened to Radio 1 top 40 charts. Heart of Glass is still number one.

Monday 12 March 1979

Stayed behind for netball. Janine rang me this evening. Watched Coronation Street. A lorry has crashed into the pub and Tracy Barlow might be dead.

Tuesday 13 March 1979

Maria brought her cassette tape recorder to school and we walked around the yard listening to Fed her on Milk and Alcohol by Dr Feelgood. Saw Susan standing outside her classroom because she talked too much again.

Wednesday 14 March 1979

Spent my savings on an Alba cassette recorder from Kays catalogue and a C60 blank tape.

Thursday 15 March 1979

Netball tournament today. Came second. Ann is very cross with Brynhyfryd school. Tried curry and rice for tea. It was nice. Banana and custard for afters. Watched Top of the Pops. Gloria Gaynor is number 1 with I Will Survive.

Friday 16 March 1979

Didn't go to piano lessons or Guides because the snow is back. We got another lamb to look after. We have named her Miss Ellie.

Saturday 17 March 1979

Babysat Laurence again this morning. Aunty Ann brought pasty and chips home from Brynithel chip shop. They were good. Then went in her car to visit her friend in Abertillery. Found out off Susan that Greg dropped my new cassette player when I was out. I am not happy. Dad is though. Wales won the rugby. JPR Williams and his team have won a Triple Crown in the Five Nations at Cardiff Arms Park.

Sunday 18th March 1979

At last, we don't have to go to Sunday School anymore. Thank goodness no more Campaigners and no more Oil in My Lamp. Went to visit Pat and Ozzie instead. Ate lots of biscuits and taped the top 40 onto my blank tape. They have a music centre with a tape deck. No background noises. It's brilliant.

Monday 19th March 1979

Mr Parfitt asked me and Ann to choose 2 more girls for gymnastic competition. We chose Helen Tucker and Catherine Courtney. We will be having gymnastic practice in dinner hour every day up until the competition which is next Friday 30th March.

Tuesday 20th March 1979

Sir told people they could come and watch us practice gymnastics. We don't think it's fair. Robert Jazzy Jarrett, Robert Nancy Young and Shaun Doughnut Martin put us off making silly faces. Catherine has left the team.

Wednesday 21st March 1979

Got a big splinter in foot from practising gymnastics with my daps off. Raquel asked Mr Parfitt to put her in the gymnastic competition. Never have I met such a cheeky girl.

Thursday 22nd March 1979

Made a cake for cake competition in Guides tomorrow. Worried about the splinter in my foot, it's too painful to bounce on the springboard and the gymnastic competition is next week.

Friday 23rd March 1979

Went to piano lessons then to Guides with my cake. Helen from up the comp was the winner. Afterwards we took the cakes up to the old people's complex and fed them to the old people there.

Saturday 24th March 1979

Good news. The splinter is out. I can carry on practising gymnastics properly now. Went over Trelewis to visit Grama and Grandad. Went with Grandad to fetch the cows in for milking. He names all his cows, they are like pets. I prefer Grandad's gentle cows to our wild horses.

Sunday 25 March 1979

Had a row with mam. We are officially enemies. There are KitKats in the tin and we can't have any. It is so unfair. I tried to walk to Grama's in Trelewis but got tired so stopped half way at Aunty Hazel's in Maesycwmmer. Had a lovely tea with French Fancy cakes. Mam and dad came to pick me up, I am in trouble now. Mam spent ages looking for me – under the beds, in the wardrobes, out the barn and everywhere. Susan was worried I had been kidnapped.

Monday 26th March 1979

Today after school I had to walk around all the fields checking on the ewes in lamb. Mam and dad said if I can walk 10 miles to Maesycwmmer then I can easily walk around the farm checking on the sheep every day after school this week. None of my friends have this much trouble over a Kitkat.

Tuesday 27th March 1979

Robert Jarrett's birthday today. Martin is getting on my nerves, he thinks he's funny singing Nice Legs Shame About Her Face at me.

Wednesday 28th March 1979

Martin has asked to go out with me and I have said yes. Stayed behind in school for more gymnastic practice. Raquel not made the team. She sulked. Had beef burger for tea.

Thursday 29th March 1979

So now the other boys are copying. John Verrier asked to go out with Janine, Robert Young with Keri G, Darryl Jones with Keri B and Gareth Larcombe with Tracy Young. The girls said yes but finished with them all by home time. Ann said no point asking her because she's going on holidays next week. We are very excited about the gymnastic competition tomorrow.

Friday 30th March 1979

Got up at 6.05, 6.30 and 7.00. Called for Ann, Helen and Keri G and went in Mr Parfitt's car to Cwmbran for the gymnastic competition. Very nervous. Watched floorwork then had sandwiches in café before our turn. Did well on tumbling but not very well on vault. Sir bought hot dogs then we went back to school. Now we have to wait for results.

Saturday 31st March 1979

Ann is going to Spain and Keri G is going to hospital. My two best friends away at the same time. Washed dishes for mam and walked Farrah and Bunty. Taped Cool for Cats onto my cassette player.

Sunday 1st April 1979

Got another lamb, this one called Bobby. Mark Peat and Robert Jarrett came to call for me. We poked sticks into cowpats. Some flicked up on Peatsy. His fringe went green and stiff, I had to take him in the house for mam to clean up before he went home.

Monday 2nd April 1979

Martin bought me a tip top and a Texan bar. Went to gymnastic club on my own because Susan has pulled a muscle in her leg doing the splits.

Tuesday 3rd April 1979

Grandad Jack is the limit. He has bought himself another crate of oranges that he won't share until they are going rotten.

Wednesday 4th April 1979

Everyone is buying Spacedust from Mrs Smith's shop and walking around the yard with heads back mouths open popping. Went down Brynithel after school and met Martin in the park. A super sunny day.

Thursday 5th April 1979

Had netball in the hall with Miss Gill. It was terrible. She was shouting all over the place. Doughnut walked past singing Georgie Best Superstar and she went mad.

Friday 6th April 1979

Keri G has had her operation and will be back in school Monday without tonsils. Went to piano lessons. Mrs Lane is lovely. I am learning to play Für Elise.

Saturday 7th April 1979

Rose the minibus came to visit with her daughter Elizabeth. She wanted to show her the lambs. Babysat Laurence again this morning. Read him lots of stories and made him giggle but I have to be careful because he gets sick when he's over excited.

Sunday 8th April 1979

Tipping down with rain. Fed the lambs and said hello to the horses then sewed eyes onto the ragdoll I am making for the Toymaker badge. Have decided to set up a club for my friends called Butterflies. I wanted to call it Pink Ladies but mam said no. Aunty Ann has told her about Grease.

Monday 9th April 1979

Bad day. Lost my leotard and my bag. Keri G was very kind and said I could borrow her shorts. Watched Chegger's Plays Pop before going to gymnastic club with Susan.

Tuesday 10th April 1979

Reading test in school. Had to wear Keri G's shorts in PE as still no leotard. Nancy came to call for me after school with Richard Miles. I think to see the lambs not me.

Wednesday 11th April 1979

Last day of school before Easter holidays. I will not see Martin for two weeks. Found out results of gymnastic competition. Ann came 39th, I came 42nd and Helen came 49th. I need to phone Ann as soon as she is back from holidays. We need to tell everyone there was 100 in the competition so they don't think we came nearly last.

Thursday 12th April 1979

Me, Susan and Greg slept over Aunty Ann's. Mam and dad were supposed to go to a dinner dance but something went wrong. Grandad Jack went to hospital. Now we can have a nice Easter. Watched Top of the Pops. Art Garfunkle is number 1 with Bright Eyes.

Friday 13th April 1979

Janine and her sister Samantha came to call for us this afternoon and we played leap frogs on the tump next to the barn. Had Cadburys cream eggs off Aunty Nellie and Uncle Idris. We phoned them to thank them.

Saturday 14th April 1979

Went to piano lessons then hurried home to change for Keri B's birthday party. Bought her a snoopy soap on a rope. Had lots to eat then a tummy ache. Keri's dad whose nickname is Snacky had to fetch me home.

Sunday 15th April 1979

Easter Sunday. Uncle Dave and Aunty Sue came to visit with Easter Eggs. We were pleased to see them. Bunty is still being hard work. I don't know if Susan will ever be able to ride her. Taped the Top 40 this evening.

Monday 16th April 1979

Visited Grama and Grandad in Trelewis. Had a nice flan for dinner. Susan and I made a tree house and met two rude boys. Went to visit Grandad Jack in hospital afterwards and stopped at a pub on the way back. We had pop and crisps in the car park.

Tuesday 17th April 1979

Spent ages juggling balls against the wall this evening. I can juggle right to the end of Knees up Mother Brown now. Susan had her best friend Natalie Howells up to play. We had a fight this evening so mam has sent us to bed early.

Wednesday 18th April 1979

The first meeting of Butterflies Club was nearly ruined by Conker's dog. It is a vicious thing called Trudy that frightens people walking up shady lane. My friends nearly went back home. Susan has gone over to Aunty Hazel's in Maesycwmmer for a holiday. I will have some peace now.

Thursday 19th April 1979

Was looking forward to a peaceful morning helping mam in the garden but Raquel popped her head over the wall and invited herself in. Trust. Went back inside and watched the Wombles with Greg.

Friday 20th April 1979

Went shopping with mam and bought Blue Jeans magazine. I was hoping to get a good pull-out poster for my wall but it was Showaddywaddy. Susan is over with Grama now. We are going to get her tomorrow.

Saturday 21st April 1979

Went over Grama's to get Susan. Grandad was on the muck and I helped pull turnips. Mam is not being very friendly to dad so he went to see Grandad Jack with his friends, Granville and Ozzie.

Sunday 22nd April 1979

Had tinned peaches with Dream Topping for tea. I wish I could have a whole packet of Dream Topping to myself. Wrote a letter to my friend Jackie Llewellyn who moved from Llanhilleth and now lives in Caerleon.

Monday 23rd April 1979

Susan has been bitten by Conker's horrible dog. She was on her way down shady lane to call for Natalie. I heard her crying all the way up back up the field. Mam had to take her for a tetanus injection. This is the second injection she's had now. Dad made her cry more by saying her bum will end up looking like a dartboard.

Tuesday 24th April 1979

Went to visit Grandad Jack. It's not good. The hospital smells funny and there is a weird man wandering around. I think I will write him a letter. Susan is getting her Homemaker badge in Brownies. She has to wash and wipe the dishes every day for a week.

Wednesday 25th April 1979

Had the second Butterflies Club meeting. Me, Janine, Debbie Tibbs and Tracy Young. Janine said we could meet at her place next time as she's getting a Soda Stream.

Thursday 26th April 1979

Was looking forward to going to the swimming baths with mam and Greg but found out that Martin and John Verrier were there. I can't swim very well and mam not at all so we would have to stay in the little pool with Greg. I went to the library instead.

Friday 27th April 1979

Went up the mountain on my bike. Dai Jones was out on his chopper. Mine is a gold Raleigh. Susan has got a red Puch but her dog bite is still sore so she stayed behind with Bunty.

Saturday 28th April 1979

Decided to be brave and said yes to going swimming with Martin and the others. We splashed around at the shallow end. It was fun. He didn't find out I can't swim. Got out at dinner time, had chips and beans, then went back in. I can put my head under water at last. But now I am in trouble for being out all day.

Sunday 29th April 1979

Doing well in piano lessons so mam said I could order a cheesecloth from Kays catalogue. Can't wait for it to come back. Went over Aunty Ann's to see Laurence.

Monday 30th April 1979

Glad to get back to school. Ann is back from her holidays in Spain with sunburn and a perm. The boys are calling her names but the girls think she looks lovely like a fashion model. She fetched us Spanish nuts to try. Mr Parfitt says they are called sunflower seeds.

Tuesday 1st May 1979

Mam took Greg to Abergavenny market and they bought chicks. The News is talking about Margaret Thatcher. Mr Parfitt was talking about her too. If she wins the election, she will be the first woman prime minister. I don't know if Mr Parfitt thinks this is a good thing or a bad thing.

Wednesday 2nd May 1979

Today was embarrassing. I had 10p to take to school. I went down Mrs Smith's shop as soon as I got off the bus and bought a mix-up and a pink panther bar but then I forgot. I went to buy crisps at tuck time and thought I had lost my money. I was upset so Mr Parfitt sent the class into the yard to help me find it and then I remembered.

Thursday 3rd May 1979

Got the ragdoll ready to take to Guides so I can get my Toymaker badge. Watched Top of the Pops. This week it was: Roxanne/the Police, Jimmy Jimmy/the Undertones, Does your Mother Know/Abba, Pop Muzik/Roxy Music. Bright Eyes is still number 1. It's so sad it makes me cry but Susan just laughs. She is mean.

Friday 4th May 1979

Went to Guides but there was none. Called for Ann instead. We were on the way to the park when we got held up by the twins. They wanted a fight. It was scary. They are tough. Thank Goodness they didn't know I had the ragdoll in my bag. Margaret Thatcher is the new prime minister.

Saturday 5th May 1979

At last Bunty has let Susan sit on her back. Visited Grandad Jack in hospital. Stopped at the pub on the way back for pop and crisps, got in really late, 11.15pm.

Sunday 6th May 1979

Tomorrow is a bank holiday and the Butterflies Club is having a treasure hunt. I spent all day making clues and hiding them around the farm. The treasure is a Cabana bar.

Monday 7th May 1979

No-one turned up for the treasure hunt but it was ok because it meant I could eat the Cabana. Grama and Grandad came to visit. Had chips and a bath.

Tuesday 8th May 1979

Today we watched a horrible safety film in school about the danger of playing near railway lines. All the girls were crying. There aren't even any railway lines near us so why did they make us watch it. On the News, 10 people died in a fire in Woolworths in Manchester. A sad day.

Wednesday 9th May 1979

Played Bulldog at breaktime with Linda Russell and Catherine Courtney. House was upside down when I got home. Mam is spring cleaning. Watched Rentaghost.

Thursday 10 May 1979

Lovely and sunny today. Played rounders in the yard at PE time. Nancy is a nuisance but a funny one. He keeps singing the Banana Splits song by the Dickies to make the girls laugh.

Friday 11th May 1979

Susan accidentally hit Tubso Young in the back of the head with a rounders ball. He turned red and charged at her like a bull. Luckily Miss Gill got there before him. Everyone was shocked at how fast she can run.

Saturday 12 May 1979

Went to piano lessons then caught the 11.15am Henleys bus to Abertillery swimming baths with Ann, Keri G and Debbie and met Martin there. We played down the shallow end and he bought me a jubbly afterwards. Some very exciting news. We are going on a holiday this summer. Mam and dad have booked a caravan at Tenby. It will be our first family holiday.

Sunday 13th May 1979

Susan has decided that Bunty is not a good name for a horse so has changed it to Emma. Aunty Lynne is coming down from England next weekend with a saddle so we can learn to ride. Arsenal beat Manchester United in the Cup final. The boys will be fighting in school tomorrow.

Monday 14th May 1979

The nit nurse was in school today. We always worry she's going to make us get undressed but luckily she only looked at our hair and our hands.

Tuesday 15th May 1979

Ann goes out with Gareth Bevan. We fetched our cassette players to school. Went down bottom steps and learned the words to Jilted John.

Wednesday 16th May 1979

Frogspawn pudding in school today with a tiny blob of jam in the middle as if this would make it better. Watched the Hair Bear Bunch and went to see Grandad Jack this evening. It is Aunty Hazel's birthday.

Thursday 17th May 1979

The boys were in trouble today. First, Doughnut and Benny tried to mutch. They went up Brynithel chip shop, bought chips and were messing about at the top of Pen-y-Graig hill, but Miss Evans saw them and brought them back in her car. Then Nancy and Verrier got into a fight and then someone scribbled on the boy's stinky toilet wall.

Friday 18th May 1979

Went to Ty'r Graig youth club. It was good. Played wrestling and weight lifting. Looked through Ann's Jackie magazine. The Boomtown Rats was in it.

Saturday 19th May 1979

Went swimming. At last had money to try one of the pies from the canteen that everyone is talking about. Martin walked me home afterwards. We saw mam and she gave him a lift back. So now Martin has met mam. She said he was a live wire. Went to visit Grama. Aunty Lynne was there with the saddle.

Sunday 20th May 1979

Helped dad this morning. Even though he is 35, he still listens to Radio 1 in his tractor.

Monday 21st May 1979

There was supposed to be a big fight between Brynithel boys and Trinant boys after school today. We could see the Trinant boys in the distance walking down their banking. The Brynithel boys walked down our banking. It took ages and everyone was fed up before they reached each other so there was no fight.

Tuesday 22nd May 1979

School sports starts this week. Me and Martin have been made girl and boy captain of Green House. Keri is vice-captain. It is a shame we are on the same team because she would make a good captain too. Ann and Peatsy are captains of Red House.

Wednesday 23rd May 1979

Mam and dad have cancelled the caravan holiday because Grandad is too ill. We will go on a day trip instead. A quiet evening. I sat in the tractor listening to Radio 1 and reading my Blue Jeans.

Thursday 24th May 1979

Jumped 3ft 7inches in high jump practice. Went to gymnastic club this evening but left early because of my leg which got hurt in the high jump. Martin has had a brace fitted on his teeth. Watched Top of the Pops. At last, a new number 1, Blondie with Sunday Girl.

Friday 25th May 1979

Jumped 3 metres in long jump practice. Susan ripped up my Blue Jeans. I am really angry with her. Went to Guides. Got my Toymaker badge at last. Then went to visit Grandad Jack.

Saturday 26th May 1979

Need to get a green t-shirt because I am in Green House. Keri G has already got hers. Ann and Maria said they are going to C&A to get boob tubes and sunglasses. I don't think they are going to win any races. Went to piano lessons.

Sunday 27th May 1979

Went to Paul's birthday party with Greg. He has written a letter to Dennis the Menace fan club and put star letter across the top. He won't believe me it's not up to him to write star letter. Taped the Top 40.

Monday 28th May 1979

Uncle Jeff and Doughnut's birthdays. I don't know why he is called Doughnut. Benny is Benny because he looks like Benny from Top Cat. Nancy is Nancy because he asked to be on the girl's netball team. But why is Doughnut Doughnut.

Tuesday 29th May 1979

Dad went to Abergavenny market. Mam is decorating. I put posters up on my wall. Mam is not happy about my Squeeze poster because the singer is wearing ripped jeans and Grama thinks it's disgraceful.

Wednesday 30th May 1979

Went up Brynithel sports field for sports day practice. Potato race and sack race went well. The three-legged race was a bit of a disaster. On the way back, Martin's mam was in the garden and he shouted 'look mam, this is my girlfriend' which was a bit embarrassing but a bit nice.

Thursday 31st May 1979

Dai Jones and Milesy came to call for me and Susan. We went tree climbing. Milesy fell out, the branch snapped, luckily he was still at the bottom. Up the Junction was on Top of the Pops. Can't believe Chas & Dave was too, Gertcha is not a proper tune. Grandad Jack has been moved to Aberbeeg hospital so is nearer us.

Friday 1st June 1979

Practised flat race. Peatsy is super-fast. Watched We are the Champions before going out in the garden to help mam. Could hear the ice-cream van down Brynithel. Wish it would come up here.

Saturday 2nd June 1979

Spent the morning with the horses then went to Janine's birthday party. Played pool. It is Aunty Ann's birthday tomorrow. Robert Jarrett is being two timed but he doesn't mind.

Sunday 3rd June 1979

Aunty Ann's birthday. Painted gates for dad this morning. Andrew Axford and Owen Price came to call for me this afternoon. We went over the tump with my cassette player.

Monday 4th June 1979

Glad to get to school. Had three sticks of rock. Ann has got a nerve, she tried to push me off my chair. Played with Leanda after school, she is very funny. Fell out of the tree and grazed my arm. Susan is very annoying, an utterly horrible ugly thing. I hate her. Grandad Jack died this morning.

Tuesday 5th June 1979

Practised ball throwing today. Keri G is amazing, she can throw loads further than the rest of us. Green House will win this one easily. Grandad Jack's funeral is Thursday. Me, Susan and Greg will be going to Rose the Minibus' house for the day.

Wednesday 6th June 1979

Me, Keri G and Ann did tuck stock take. Burtons smokey bacon piglets have come in. We had to get the boxes from Mr Phelps' office. We saw his cane. Glad I'm not one of the boys. Getting the dap off Mrs Bray was bad enough for playing tag on the tables.

Thursday 7th June 1979

Grandad Jack's funeral. Susan and I stayed at Rose the minibus' house. We played with Mandy and her skateboard. Lots of visitors when we got back. It is a sad day. Tubeway Army, the Tourists and Elvis Costello was on Top of the Pops.

Friday 8th June 1979

Ann wore her new dunkie jacket to school. Susan and Miss Gill make a right pair. Both annoying.

Saturday 9th June 1979

No piano lessons today. Me and Susan picked stones over the opencast instead. Dad parked up the tractor and trailer and put the radio on for us. I was one side and she was the other. We kept missing the trailer and whizzing stones past each other's heads. Earned 50p each.

Sunday 10th June 1979

Made rock cakes this morning then Martin came to call for me this afternoon. We made a tree house and put a swing up. I took my cassette player with us.

Monday 11th June 1979

We have got a colour TV. Watched the Waltons in colour on BBC2. Then tennis. Bjorn Borg won. Then the News. John Wayne the cowboy died.

Tuesday 12th June 1979

Went to youth club and played on the trampette. Me and Ann broke friends, and Keri G and Keri B had a fight. Went down the infants to help with the milk again. Crates of the stuff, warm from being left outside in the sun with a yellow layer of cream at the top. Yuk.

Wednesday 13th June 1979

Big fights in the yard. Me and Ann. My side had the most because I had all Susan's friends too. Keri G isn't as nice as I thought she was. She went on Ann's side and charged at me with a tennis racket. Debbie gone mean too. Mrs Sellick was running around like a chicken with its head off.

Thursday 14th June 1979

Our class went up the comp for a look around today. The teachers look strict. I will miss Mr Parfitt. Everyone is saying the first years will get their heads flushed down the toilet by the second years. It is worrying. Watched Top of the Pops. A terrible new number 1. Anita Ward with You Can Ring My Bell.

Friday 15th June 1979

Debbie is still being mean. Martin went to see her in Mr Reed's class but got dragged back out by his ear. Mr Reed wouldn't even let him explain why he was there.

Saturday 16th June 1979

Aberbeeg fete today. I went with Janine. Lovely and sunny. Mam has bought us summer coats. A cagoule for me, a dunkie jacket for Susan and a bomber jacket for Greg. (Note: Mam returned Susan's jacket to the shop before she had chance to wear it. Someone must have told her.)

Sunday 17th June 1979

Me and Greg went over Aunty Ann's. Greg stayed there all day. Having a colour TV is really good. Even Songs of Praise was interesting.

Monday 18th June 1979

Back to school. Everyone is friends again. There has been a boyfriend swap. Ann now with Nancy, Keri G back with John Verrier, Keri B with Robert Jarrett and Janine with Darryl Jones. It is very sunny. I have a heat bump. Waiting for chance to wear my new cagoule.

Tuesday 19th June 1979

We might be getting a new landrover. It is exciting but I would prefer if we could get something more fashionable for a change like a Ford Cortina or a Morris Marina. So we can have proper seats in the back.

Wednesday 20th June 1979

Sports day tomorrow. Was planning to spend my stone-picking money in Woolies on something green for Green House but left it too late. The shops are shut on Wednesdays.

Thursday 21st June 1979

Sports day. It rained but at least I got chance to wear my new cagoule. I came 1st, 1st, 2nd and 3rd. Keri G done well too but Red House still won. Ann and Peatsy were happy. Green came 2nd. Karen's ear was bleeding because Julie pulled it so hard.

Friday 22nd June 1979

A very lovely day. It was the school trip to Longleat. There were lots to see. We went on paddle boat rides. Me and Martin, Ann and Nancy but we have to stop calling him Nancy because Ann isn't happy about it, and Keri G and Darryl. Someone stole 50p. Mr Parfitt took us home afterwards.

Saturday 23rd June 1979

I went to piano lessons then me, Ann and Janine made a good grass slide down the banking. Susan went to call for her friends. Walked the horses this evening. We are getting them used to wearing the saddle but Emma is still a problem.

Sunday 24th June 1979

Martin and Youngy came to call for me this morning, we went tree climbing. Had a bath this evening and watched the Mallens about a man with a white streak in his hair. It was good.

Monday 25th June 1979

Played elastics in the yard today. Inter Schools Sports Day is on Thursday at Abertillery Park. We need to beat our enemy, Brynhyfryd. Mam is making jam.

Tuesday 26th June 1979

Gina Dewfall's birthday party. The cake was lovely. We played games. Kelly's Eye was good. We were blindfolded then made to stick our finger in jelly which we thought was an eyeball. Then we were blindfolded again and had to taste different food like mustard and guess what it was. Ann and Maria were doing a weird dance that they have seen on Top of the Pops.

Wednesday 27th June 1979

The boys are talking about Muhammad Ali the boxer. He has finished boxing. Dad likes Johnny Owen the Merthyr Matchstick. I prefer watching Giant Haystacks and Big Daddy. Watched 'Go with Noakes', he was in the Scottish Highlands with his dog Shep.

Thursday 28th June 1979

Inter Schools Sports Day at Abertillery Park. Ty'r Graig came 4th. Brynhyfryd beat us. There was lots of cheating going on. Especially Swffryd School in the sack race. Robert Jarrett was upset, he'd been practising hard. We have got a new landrover. Aunty Ann is thrilled. Watched Top of the Pops. Tubeway Army with Are Friends Electric is number 1.

Friday 29th June 1979

We went in the new landrover to visit Grama and Grandad in Trelewis. Grama has been to the charity shops again and bought us some awful clothes. Went up the duckpond with Grandad. We like his funny stories.

Saturday 30th June 1979

Our cousin Jayne from Nelson came to visit. We went on our bikes up the canyon. I took the bend too fast and went straight down the bank. My clothes are ripped, I've got gorse bush splinters stuck everywhere and my wheel is buckled. Susan and Jayne had to help me home even though they are both younger than me. Not a good day.

Sunday 1 July 1979

We have got sheep shearers from New Zealand coming to help with the shearing next weekend. Started to tape the Top 40 this evening but tape got mangled. Tried to straighten it out but now it is just a spaghetti mess. Have decided to spend my savings on a new C120.

Monday 2nd July 1979

Martin has had a haircut. Me and Greg went over Aunty Ann's after school. Greg played up and Laurence is off his food.

Tuesday 3rd July 1979

Ann is not my friend again. Don't ask me why. I felt like bashing her face in.

Wednesday 4th July 1979

The cat has had kittens. Me and Susan watched the Liverbirds this evening because mam was down the garden and forgot about the time.

Thursday 5th July 1979

Youngy's birthday. Dad is busy gathering sheep ready for shearing and mam is making pasties. Born to Be Alive and Dave Edmunds with Girls Talk was on Top of the Pops.

Friday 6th July 1979

The sheep shearers have arrived. One is a huge Maori and the other is smaller and white but still from New Zealand. The new landrover is dirty already and the house smells of sheep. Me and Susan will be helping tomorrow.

Saturday 7th July 1979

Me and Susan helped with the shearing. Our job was to brush the loose wool away from around the shearers' feet.

The Maori's feet were huge. He wore flip flops. Susan kept accidentally stabbing his toes with her bristle brush but he was very friendly. Mam said he was a gentleman because he gave himself a hosepipe shower in the yard before coming in the house for dinner.

Sunday 8th July 1979

Had a good look through Kays catalogue. Me and Susan are going to order towelling pyjamas for mam for her birthday. They cost £10.79. We will have finished paying by her birthday which is 24th October.

Monday 9th July 1979

Mr Parfitt has said we can put on a concert in the hall for the juniors on our last week of school. The girls had a meeting. Me, Ann, Keri G and Keri B are going to sing Sunday Girl and Oliver's Army. Linda Russell says she knows all the words to Don't Jump Off the Roof Dad so she's going to sing that one and Judith Humphreys knows Billericay Dickie so she's doing that. We are going to start practising tomorrow.

Tuesday 10th July 1979

So now the boys are planning a concert too. There is a Skylab falling from space. The News says it's over 70 ton and could kill people. It was quite scary being out in the yard at breaktimes.

Wednesday 11th July 1979

The Skylab has landed in the Indian Ocean. It is a relief.
Martin had a row off Mr Phelps today. His face goes purple
when he shouts. Poor Martin. Ann came up this evening
and Susan is bad.

Thursday 12th July 1979

We sneaked a look at the boys practising their concert.
They were singing the Sex Pistols C'mon Everybody. It was
terrible. Dazzy Morgan was teaching them how to pogo.
They were jumping up and down so much that they were
too out of breath to sing and they weren't keeping together
with the words. Dad has started hay baling Church Meadow.

Friday 13th July 1979

The boys have changed their minds about doing a concert
so it's just us after all. Had a letter off my friend Jackie
Llewellyn who moved from Llanhilleth to Caerleon. Mam
says I can invite her to stay in the summer holidays. Watched
the Goodies this evening.

Saturday 14th July 1979

Me and Susan helped with the hay baling. Our job is to roll
the bales together to make stacks. It was hot and our arms
are scratched. But it's better than potato picking.

Sunday 15th July 1979

Very sunny. Tried sunbathing up the garden but it didn't work, still white. Jackie Llewellyn is coming to stay on 3rd August. I can't wait. The last time we saw each other was when we were seven.

Monday 16th July 1979

Me and Ann sunbathed in the yard at dinnertime but Mrs Sellick and Mrs Hancock made us put our tops back on. They are a pair of grumps. Concert coming good.

Tuesday 17th July 1979

The concert is tomorrow. We have decided to wear shorts, punk shirts, ties and sunglasses. Linda and Judith are wearing their jumpsuits with the trousers legs rolled up. We practised all afternoon. Me and Keri B had a fight.

Wednesday 18th July 1979

We done the concert. Sunday Girl, Oliver's Army, Don't jump off the Roof Dad and Billericay Dickie. Keri G wore the wrong top and I wore tights under my shorts which was a bad idea because I was sliding all over the place on the wooden stage. Linda and Judith were really good. We think everyone enjoyed it.

Thursday 19th July 1979

We are allowed to fetch games to school for the last two days. Maria fetched her cassette player and we played Chartbuster. Darts, UK Subs, The Knack, Sparks and the Boomtown Rats were on Top of the Pops.

Friday 20th July 1979

Last day at Ty'r Graig school. Finished with Martin as there's no point. I will miss Mr Parfitt, he has been my favourite teacher ever. Nigel Creed got to ring the home time bell for the very last time.

Saturday 21st July 1979

Spent the morning with the kittens and the horses then went over Grama and Grandad in Trelewis. I am deciding whether to get pies or pasties to wear up the comp.

Sunday 22nd July 1979

Looking forward to the Royal Welsh Show in 3 days' time. It's where we go every year for our daytrip. It was the last episode of the Mallens this evening.

Monday 23rd July 1979

Grandad's birthday. Watched creepy Mr Noseybonk and silly Captain Pugwash before going to gymnastic club. Mr C said I am now good enough to go to Sunday Club gymnastics at Roseheyworth.

Tuesday 24th July 1979

Took lambs to Abergavenny market. Bought things ready for comp. Navy blue jumper, navy blue skirt and pies. Got Kit Kats and nice things to go in our sandwiches to take to the Royal Welsh Show tomorrow. We have got pups.

Wednesday 25th July 1979

Went to the Royal Welsh Show. Wore my new pies. Greg kept getting lost. Seen a massive bull. Went on the flying jets. Bought a pot of pink slime with plastic worms in. Uncle Gwyn is staying with us.

Thursday 26th July 1979

Dad's birthday and also Dai Jones' from over the pub. Me and Susan went over Aunty Ann's to show her the slime. There wasn't anyone in the kitchen so we thought it would be a good joke to tip it out on the floor. It didn't go well. She came back in and went mad on the dog, she thought he had been sick.

Friday 27th July 1979

Greg went to Bristol Zoo with Aunty Ann, Uncle Jeff and Laurence. Me and Susan walked Farrah and Emma with mam. One of the kittens has gone missing.

Saturday 28th July 1979

Trouble over Aunty Ann's again. Greg burst into her kitchen pretending to be a monkey wearing his monkey mask from Bristol Zoo and terrified Laurence who was sat in his highchair eating his breakfast. Went to piano lessons.

Sunday 29th July 1979

Went to Sunday gymnastic club up Roseheyworth. Taped the Top 40. I love the new number 1, The Boomtown Rats with I don't like Mondays. Aunty Ann is going on holidays.

Monday 30th July 1979

Mam has put a bar up out the garden so me and Susan can practise wrap arounds. Went with dad up to Mrs Morgan's. My job was to open the gates for the landrover to drive through because there were lots of them. The dogs were so smelly in the back that I could hardly breathe.

Tuesday 31st July 1979

Decorated my half of the bedroom ready for Jackie Llewellyn's visit. Have painted it blue. Susan went down Brynithel and bought refreshers. Watched Sapphire and Steel.

Wednesday 1st August 1979

Painted my bedside cabinet and put a Boomtown Rats poster up on my wall. I hope Jackie will like everything. Practised wrap arounds on the bar in the garden and went down Brynithel to get bread for mam.

Thursday 2nd August 1979

Rang Jackie to find out what time she will be arriving tomorrow. Aunty Lynne came for tea and took Susan back with her to England. Sham 69 with Hersham Boys, BA Robertson with Bang Bang, the Specials with Gangsters and Legs & Co were on Top of the Pops.

Friday 3rd August 1979

Jackie Llewellyn has come to stay. She is quieter than I remember but I expect it's just that she's feeling shy. I am very excited. Her dad and her sister Karen dropped her off. Karen had a dark-skinned friend with her.

Saturday 4th August 1979

Jackie is very good with horses. We took a picnic up the mountain on the bikes. We saw a dead sheep. Jackie was shocked and poked it with a stick. We helped dad with the haymaking this evening.

Sunday 5th August 1979

Jackie felt more at home today. We started a jigsaw and let Greg bother with us. We took her back home this evening and then called in to see Uncle Dave and Aunty Sue who live nearby.

Monday 6th August 1979

Raining. Watched Roobarb & Custard and played railways with Greg. Finished the jigsaw. Broke the calculator. Watched Nationwide. Made the mistake of saying I was bored so now mam is writing list of jobs for me to do tomorrow. Trust.

Tuesday 7th August 1979

Done jobs. Choose one 10p one and three 5p ones so earned 25p altogether. Started reading Six Bad Boys by Enid Blyton. Watched Blue Peter Special Assignment. Peter Purves was in France.

Wednesday 8th August 1979

Went shopping with mam to buy the rest of my school uniform. A yellow Trutex top and black shorts for PE. Sprayed some Babe perfume from the tester bottle in one of the shops. Never have I smelled anything so good apart from Playdough.

Thursday 9th August 1979

Finished reading Six Bad Boys by Enid Blyton and started What Katy Did Next by Susan Coolidge. Watched Top of the Pops. Reasons to be Cheerful by Ian Dury and the Blockheads, Money by the Flying Lizards, the Diary of Horace Wimp by ELO and Is She Really Going Out with Him by Joe Jackson was on there. The News says a nudist beach in Brighton has opened. An embarrassing holiday that would be.

Friday 10th August 1979

Went to Abertillery shopping with mam and Greg. Got my Blue Jeans then went back to the landrover to read it. Ronnie the tractor sales rep was here when we got back. Dad's tractor is posh, it has heating, a radio and a big spongy seat. Mam has to put up with our old settee.

Saturday 11th August 1979

Grama's birthday. She came up this afternoon and mam made a nice tea. Grandad crawled under the windowsill holding a stick with his hat on it so it looked like a very short man was walking past. He always does a joke when he arrives.

Sunday 12th August 1979

Cleaned the landrover to earn pocket money then went over Aunty Ann's. She had a nice holiday. Talked to Susan on the phone this evening. She is having fun in England with Sorrell the horse, Aunty Lynne has trained her well. Watched the Onedin Line.

Monday 13th August 1979

Bad day for mam. She tried to lead Emma around church meadow but Emma took off. Dad was shouting for her to hang on and his friend Granville was shouting to let go. She hung on for a while, got dragged on her belly through cowpats, is bruised but ok.

Tuesday 14th August 1979

Mam went to Newport with Aunty Ann and Uncle Jeff. I minded Greg and Laurence. Mam bought me a leather satchel for comp. I am worried. Everyone else said they were getting adidas sports bags. I might be the only one with a leather satchel.

Wednesday 15th August 1979

Had a big bowl of butterscotch flavour Ready Brek for breakfast and then went to visit Frank England with mam. I prefer butter flavour, wish they would bring it back. Greg is amazing. He has read the Faraway Tree in two days. He is only 5.

Thursday 16th August 1979

Took a Buzby badge over for Laurence. Minded him while Aunty Ann made a coffee flavour cheesecake. It was delicious. Started Reading the Secret Garden by Frances Hodgson Burnett. There was no Top of the Pops because of a strike. Susan is coming home tomorrow.

Friday 17th August 1979

Mam and dad went over Hafodrynys to meet Aunty Lynne for the handover of Susan. She fetched back presents. I had sweets and a ring. I was very pleased. They didn't get back until 10.40pm. I was nervous. I tried to watch the telly but BBC was boring and there was a blank screen on HTV because it's on strike.

Saturday 18th August 1979

Today is my holiday at Jackie's house in Caerleon. It is nice here. Jackie and her sister Karen are very fashionable. Their mam and dad went out and left Karen in charge of us. We had coke and crisps and stayed up until midnight.

Sunday 19th August 1979

Got up at 10.30am. The longest lie in I have ever had. Had a game of scrabble and listened to Dollar. Went to Bristol Zoo this afternoon and then visited Jackie's aunty and walked her dogs.

Monday 20th August 1979

Got up at 10.15am. We went to the swimming baths then to the Green which is patch of grass in the middle of Caerleon where people hang about. Karen was talking to a boy called Matthew. Came home this evening. I have had a lovely holiday.

Tuesday 21st August 1979

Mam went to Abergavenny market. Aunty Ann had a Tupperware party over her house.

Wednesday 22nd August 1979

Phoned Ann up. We went swimming. Took Susan. It was good but we made an enemy in the pool. Cliff Richard is in the top 10 with We Don't Talk Anymore. He is 38, older than dad, I don't think he should be allowed in the charts.

Thursday 23rd August 1979

The pups chased the chickens, there was clucking and feathers everywhere. Blue makes the bedroom feel cold. We will need to paint it again before winter. Watched Top of the Pops. Cliff Richard has made it to number 1. Terrible.

Friday 24th August 1979

Mrs Lane my piano teacher rang up. No lessons tomorrow. Mam went shopping and got my comp tie. Hung everything up in my wardrobe ready for next Monday. Mam has sewn name tags on everything. My wardrobe smells of satchel.

Saturday 25th August 1979

Laurence is sleeping over our house tonight because Aunty Ann and Uncle Jeff have gone somewhere. Dad was good fun, he tried doing gymnastics and got stuck doing the cradle. Watched the Hardy Boys and Nancy Drew Mysteries this afternoon because it was raining outside.

Sunday 26th August 1979

Arthur Watts came to visit with his grandchildren. He was wearing the biggest pies I have ever seen. Aunty Ann went to Barry Island. Mam took me to Grama and Grandad in Trelewis. I am staying here all week.

Monday 27th August 1979

Went with Grandad to get his morning newspaper and Woodbine cigarettes. He bought me a box of candy ones. Helped him with the milking. Daisy and Buttercup are my favourite. An important person has been murdered on his boat. His name is Lord Mount Batten. Grandad said it was an IRA bomb.

Tuesday 28th August 1979

It is very sunny. Aunty Hazel and Uncle Kevin picked me up and took me to the River Usk. The cafe was full so we went back to their house in Maesycwmmer and had vesta curry and toffee ice-cream. I loved it. I am staying here tonight.

Wednesday 29th August 1979

Still sunny. Uncle Kevin dropped me off at the Ffladcaiach Inn and I walked back up to Grama and Grandad. Greg rang me to say he has read another one of my books, Enid Blyton The Wishing Chair. I have got some spangles to take back for him and Susan, and also a pet hedgehog.

Thursday 30th August 1979

Helped Grandad clean the dairy with his helper called David. Mam came over to pick me up, her and Grama are both in a mood today. Watched Top of the Pops. Duchess by the Stranglers and Gangsters by the Specials was on there.

Friday 31st August 1979

Minded Laurence. He played up a bit, he was not his usual self. Uncle Jeff was getting his onions ready for Brynithel show tomorrow. Mam went shopping and fetched Blue Jeans for me, Bunty for Sue, Beano for Greg and Farmers Weekly for dad. Disappointing poster in Blue Jeans this week, Dukes of Hazzard.

Saturday 1st September 1979

Today was Brynithel Vegetable Show. Mam had 1st prize with her potatoes and runner beans. Uncle Jeff had 1st prize with his beetroot. Susan had 2nd prize with her miniature garden which she made on our turkey plate but it was nearly disqualified. Lisa Morgan's nan reported mam for fiddling with it but mam was only tidying it up because the dog had jumped on it in the back of the landrover. Lisa won 1st prize so her nan was happy then.

Sunday 2nd September 1979

Today is the last day of the summer holidays. Tomorrow is the first day of Comp. I feel sick. Had a bath. Me and Susan had a fight. Mam cut my hair. Dad watched the cricket. Listened to Top 40.

Monday 3rd September 1979

Started Comp. Me and Ann have been put together. Keri G is next door. Everyone is spread out. It is a shame we are not altogether. Milesy and Verrier have gone to different schools. There is an unusual boy in our class called Tecwyn and a boy who looks like trouble called Timothy. Mrs English is our form teacher, she seems nice.

Tuesday 4th September 1979

There are some scary teachers in this school. So far, we have met Mr Maths, Madame French, Mrs RE and Mr Chemistry. I don't think any of them likes kids much. Our homework this evening was to cover our books. I used left over wallpaper from the living room. It took ages. I think Ann might be a bit jealous of my satchel.

Wednesday 5th September 1979

Today was PE. We went swimming. Miss PE is the scariest teacher yet. I made a fool of myself. My swimming costume is old fashioned and I didn't realise until it was too late. It's got a skirt thing and a boat on it. Everyone else has speedos.

We had to swim a width so we could be put into groups. I splashed more than I swam, everyone laughed, I have been put in the beginners group. I wish I had practised more in the summer holidays.

Thursday 6th September 1979

Made some new friends. Jacquelyn Butler from Brynhyfryd, Claire Mitchell, Claire Giles and Cauline Lewis from Queen Street. Had needlework and music. Our needlework teacher is called Bunhead and our music teacher is called Fanny. A lot of the teachers have nicknames here. Joined the school choir because we didn't have a choice. I am very tired.

Friday 7th September 1979

Had physics and geography today. The physic teacher's name is Bulldog. Mrs Geography is very stern and wears glasses too big for her head. I am not too fond of this school. Practiced the piano this evening and watched Carry on Screaming.

Saturday 8th September 1979

Mam has bought me a new swimming costume. Went to piano lessons then went swimming with Ann and her cousin. Practised hard. Watched That's Life with Esther Rantzen this evening.

Sunday 9th September 1979

The Yorkshire Ripper has killed another woman. The News says it is not safe for women to go out by themselves. I am not looking forward to going to school tomorrow.

Monday 10th September 1979

There is a boy in our class who is a massive bighead. His name is Alan Jones but everyone calls him Bus because of Jones' buses in Aberbeeg. Mrs Geography went mad on him because he wrote on his geography book – Alan Jones year 1 could be in year 2 good enough to be in year 3.

Tuesday 11th September 1979

Horrible day. Mr Chemistry is the most horriblest man. He sits with his feet up on his desk flicking his ruler. Art class was ok. Mr Art doesn't talk much, he just smokes Embassys, but it was good fun drawing people at a bus stop.

Wednesday 12th September 1979

Miss History, what a nice teacher. It's a shame we got Mr History instead, although he's quite nice as well. Found Maria Stocker who I went to Six Bells nursery with and Kay who I used to sit by before she moved from Ty'r Graig to Brynhyfryd.

Thursday 13th September 1979

Forgot to take my English homework to school. I was scared but Mrs English was nice about it. Thank goodness it wasn't my French homework. Madame French is crazy. 'Speak now or forever hold your wotzits' she keeps saying. Makes us laugh though. Miss PE made us do cross country running around the Glebe park.

Friday 14th September 1979

Another mess up. I thought it was home time and went to wait for the bus but no-one else was there. Walked back up to school and found the rest of my class in the biology portacabin having last lesson. I didn't get into trouble for being late though, everyone laughed, even Miss Biology. I am glad it is Friday.

Saturday 15th September 1979

Dad went to a sheep sale. He was going to fetch crisps back for us but we fell asleep before he got home. Watched Top Cat with Greg this morning, went with Susan to see the horses this afternoon, and watched the Generation Game this evening. Mam has cut her hair, I don't like it.

Sunday 16th September 1979

Mam, Susan, Greg and I walked down the forestry at the back of Six Bells to Abertillery Swimming baths. I wore my new costume. Listened to the Top 40 this evening. Sadly, Cliff Richards is still number 1.

Monday 17th September 1979

Back to school. Went to gymnastic club this evening but it takes so long getting home from school I don't know if I can keep going. Me and Dai Jones have to wait outside Hammonds shop in Brynithel for Rose the Minibus to come get us after the school bus has dropped us off. We were there ages today and I was hungry and Hammonds shop is full of nice things. Keri G came out of her house to keep us company.

Tuesday 18th September 1979

Had fun shrinking crisp packets on the heating vents in the yard today. Greg brought his friend Mark home from school. He didn't invite him, he just came. Elaine's wedding is on Saturday.

Wednesday 19th September 1979

Timothy Edwards and Andrew Bull were annoying today. They think they are the Likely Lads or something. Dai Jones brought his magic tricks to school. It helped the time go quicker waiting for Rose the Minibus outside Hammonds.

Thursday 20th September 1979

Henleys sent one of its old cronky buses to take us home from school. It cronked and squeaked all the way up Cemetery Road. I hope we get our usual one back tomorrow so we can listen to radio one.

Friday 21st September 1979

Mam went to Abergavenny. She bought new shoes for Elaine's wedding and went to a proper hairdresser. Her hair looks lovely now. The photographer came to school and we had a class photo done.

Saturday 22nd September 1979

Mam and dad went to Elaine's wedding. Me, Susan and Greg stayed with Pat and Ozzie in Glandwr Street. Leanda came too. Took my C120 so I could tape Radio 1 from the tape deck on their music centre. It's brilliant not getting background noises. Got Rainbow Since You've Been Gone, Roxy Music Angel Eyes, ELO Don't Bring Me Down, Nick Lowe Cruel to be Kind. Then we walked up to Abertillery Park and watched a rugby match.

Sunday 23rd September 1979

Rained all day. Looked through Kays catalogue and did maths homework. Mam forgot to buy cat food so we ran out. Listened to Top 40. Hurrah. A new number 1. Gary Numan with Cars. Tony Blackburn has taken over from Simon Bates.

Monday 24th September 1979

Miss PE picked me and Keri G to go in the cross-country competition. She can't remember our names so she calls us both Dina. HTV is STILL on strike. Fed up of just watching BBC.

Tuesday 25th September 1979

Trouble between Miss PE and Madame French. Miss PE came into French class and told me to come out and practise cross country. Madame French told her to get lost. They argued. I didn't know whether to stand up or sit down. Madame French won, I stayed in French class. Told mam. Said they had been a fight in school. She said teachers need to sort the kids out, had to explain it wasn't the kids, it was the teachers.

Wednesday 26th September 1979

Had the posh Henleys bus with the nice radio to take us to school this morning. We listened to the Radio 1 Breakfast show with the Hairy Cornflake, Dave Lee Travis. Art today. We had to draw the inside of an antique shop.

Thursday 27th September 1979

Our prime minister does not seem to be very popular. She does not seem to be very kind to people. Me and Ann walked down to Protheroes shop at dinner time. We didn't have any money but it was a nice walk. Watched Top of the Pops this evening. The Police are number 1 with Message in a Bottle.

Friday 28th September 1979

PE today. Practised for the cross-country competition. Went down Brynithel after school but had to come back home before I got there because I noticed mam had ironed a crease in my jeans which is not cool.

Saturday 29th September 1979

Watched a bit of Swap Shop then went to Mrs Lane's for my piano lesson. Her grandchildren were there. Called into Aunty Ann's on my way back. Starsky and Hutch was on this evening.

Sunday 30th September 1979

Me and Susan cleaned the landrover to earn some pocket money and listened to the Noel Edmonds Sunday Morning Show on the radio. A good new song out, Video Killed the Radio Star by the Buggles.

Monday 1st October 1979

Today is my birthday! I had a Blue Jeans Annual off mam and green cords off Aunty Ann but they didn't fit so she gave them to Susan. Ran into a wall in school and nearly knocked myself out because the boys were chasing me to give me the bumps and then fainted in assembly. Spent the morning in the medical room. Ann and Maria bought me presents and mam made me a lovely tea when I got home from school. A very nice day.

Tuesday 2nd October 1979

Had a late birthday card off Jackie Llewelyn and the right size cords off Aunty Ann. Cookery lesson today was about hygiene. We learnt to clean our teeth properly and how to clean our hairbrushes.

Wednesday 3rd October 1979

Can't believe Fanny. I thought music would be my favourite lesson but all she does is talk about Peter and the flippin wolf. Maureen Hockey and Helen Durham are going to have trumpet lessons. Fanny does not seem interested that I am learning to play the piano.

Thursday 4th October 1979

Ann and Maria had curry and chips from Market Street chip shop at dinner time. They were stonking. Wish I could take money instead of sandwiches.

Friday 5th October 1979

Mam went to a meeting in Ty'r Graig about Susan. Her teacher has been telling witch stories and Susan can't get to sleep at night anymore. Dai Jones is getting madder and madder with Dilwyn who is on the same minibus as us. He keeps making fun of people. If he's not careful, he will get duffed up.

Saturday 6th October 1979

Went to piano lessons. Doughnut, Benny and Vic were in the park. Well Shaun, Lee and Philip really but no-one calls them that. I was surprised to see Doughnut as Mrs Lane said he was going for his lesson after me. He's already been in trouble once before for bunking off and spending his 50p on football stickers. Susan went to Catherine Frazer's birthday party and I went with dad to save him having to get out of the landrover to open the gates.

Sunday 7th October 1979

Went over Aunty Ann's but she was in a bad mood so came back home. Mam made chelsea buns. Delicious. Got a bad stomach this evening. I hope I don't have to go to school tomorrow. Taped the Top 40.

Monday 8th October 1979

Miss PE was ill today so some of us had to go in Madame French's class instead. I felt sorry for one of the year 3 boys. He was being cheeky so Madame French put her jumper over his head and nearly suffocated him with her big boobs.

Tuesday 9th October 1979

Laurence is 3 today. Dai Jones is busy plotting his plan. There is going to be trouble on the minibus. Mr Chemistry ate a tub of cottage cheese with pineapple in class again today.

Wednesday 10th October 1979

Today I was moved up from beginners group in swimming. Hurray. On the way home from school, me and Ann was talking to a boy from the 3rd year. His name is Chris Townsend.

Thursday 11th October 1979

We watched Chris Townsend play football in the yard. He is good. Dai Jones chickened out of his plan on the minibus so Dilwyn got away with poking fun of everyone again. Watched Top of the Pops. The Devil Went Down to Georgia, Tusk and OK Fred this week.

Friday 12th October 1979

Dai carried out his plan. It was a shame because Dilwyn didn't actually say anything today so Dai is now in big trouble for starting a fight over nothing. As soon as the minibus reached the pump house, he got out of his seat and punched him. Rose nearly crashed into the bank. She threw Dai off the bus and he had to walk home. Poor Dai. This evening the parents rowed. Me and Susan were called to explain what had been happening. Dilwyn's mam called us liars. We cried all the way across the lane, we are so angry, it's so unfair. Dad had to nearly sit on mam to stop her going back over.

Saturday 13th October 1979

Andrew Bevan and his friend came to call for us this afternoon and we played conkers. Andrew was wearing bovver boots. I am wearing my bobble hat to bed tonight to see if it will make my hair straight.

Sunday 14th October 1979

Took Laurence for a walk. It is my American cousin's birthday today. Her name is Gwyneth because her mother is from Wales. Watched Roots this evening, about Kunta Kinte, Kizzy and Chicken George.

Monday 15th October 1979

Fed up of school. The best bit is the bus. Had needlework. Bunhead was in a bad mood. Started to make an octopus. Mine went wrong. Making oven gloves instead. Blue Peter's 21st birthday.

Tuesday 16th October 1979

Me and Ann took our cookery baskets to school. We made biscuits. Was looking forward to eating them at break time but my basket got locked in the cookery room. Me and Ann tried to get in through the window but couldn't.

Wednesday 17th October 1979

Aunty Lynne's birthday in England. The school was going on a trip to France but not enough people are going so it has been cancelled. The boys were talking about 'Not the Nine O'clock News' on the bus. Had pork for dinner.

Thursday 18th October 1979

Ann fancies herself as a gymnast and everyone believes her. I went to gymnastic club after school but there wasn't any. Top of the Pops was good. Video Killed the Radio Star has made it to number 1.

Friday 19th October 1979

Me and Susan are going to earn extra pocket money by selling vegetables from the garden to the neighbours. We went to Catman's house, we haven't seen his mother before because she's old and stuck in the house. She bought everything in our basket. She is nice but she talked for a whole hour, our feet were aching and we were worried we would end up smelling of cats.

Saturday 20th October 1979

I am learning to play duets on the piano with Mrs Lane. Susan's friends, Helen and Michelle, came to call for her but didn't stay long because Michelle rocked so hard on the rocking chair that it catapulted her onto the floor. She went home crying.

Sunday 21st October 1979

Went over Aunty Ann's and played hide and seek with Laurence. Taped the Top 40 this evening. Making Plans for Nigel by XTC makes me laugh. It reminds me of Nigel Creed, the coolest boy in our year.

Monday 22nd October 1979

Half term. The new Kays catalogue has come. Greg is not well. Catman really got on my nerves today. He was walking up the hill the same time as me. He said you're all putting on weight over there, if you carry on you'll be like a family of flumps. I told mam.

Tuesday 23rd October 1979

Susan's birthday. She is now 10. She had a Bunty Annual, a Mars bar and £1. We are going to have a joint birthday party on Halloween. She went to a jumble sale down Brynithel with mam. Dad went to market and Greg was sick.

Wednesday 24th October 1979

Mam's birthday. She is now 34. Dad remembered to buy a card this year but he didn't write on it because it said 'to my wife' on the front so he thought he didn't need to say who it was off. Mam says she is giving up. She took Greg to the doctors. HTV is back. It was good to watch Coronation Street again.

Thursday 25th October 1979

Babysat Laurence. Aunty Ann came back with chips. Watched Top of the Pops, Blankety Blank and Citizen Smith. Really bad number 1, One Day at a Time, Lena Martell.

Friday 26th October 1979

Me and Susan made Halloween lanterns out of swedes ready for our party. Sold vegetables to the neighbours again. Mrs Williams bought most this week and we made 22½ pence each. Watched Crackerjack.

Saturday 27th October 1979

Went over Grama and Grandad in Trelewis. Grama made a nice flan. Practised piano. Grama's piano is a lot better than ours, the keys come straight back up after you press them.

Sunday 28th October 1979

Revised for maths test. Made another lantern for the party. Susan got chased by Raquel's dog. There is now a nasty dog to walk past whichever way we go down to Brynithel. Listened to the top 40. All the boys like the same song, Whatever You Want, Status Quo.

Monday 29th October 1979

Had maths test. Watched Angels, my favourite programme, it's about nurses. Mam is busy wallpapering. Owen Price is getting very tall. He has a new name. Growen Owen.

Tuesday 30th October 1979

We are learning to play the recorder in Music. It is not a good noise. Biology was good because Miss Biology wasn't there so we didn't have a lesson. Raquel is being a proper madam.

Wednesday 31st October 1979

We had our Halloween party in the front room. It was fancy dress. I wore Greg's monkey mask and a black blanket. Keri G wore a blanket too. Susan wore her welsh hat and I loaned Janine mine. Greg wore a bin bag. Ann and Maria had witch's masks, they looked fabulous. Susan's friends got here first. My friends were late but we could hear them coming up Shady Lane screaming. Robert Jazzy Jarrett was scaring them, the boys were coming up too, not to the party but to the Old Church. Mam made pasties and fancy cakes for the party, everyone loved them. Played 'ducking apple'. Helen got soaked and was crying. Played 'things on strings' and Keri B bite into a bar of soap. She was nearly crying too until mam told her she could take the soap home with her, she was happy then. Ann got a bit bossy and Samantha and Natalie ought to be ashamed of their behaviour but we all had a brilliant time. But there was trouble afterwards. We wanted to go over the churchyard, there was loads of people from school there. Mam said we could go over to wave friends off and come straight back. But Greg ran off, there was a small hole in the church door and the older boys were encouraging him to squeeze through. I was really scared. But then everyone moved down the road to Raquel's house and started singing Murphy Mint really loud outside her gate. She has got on everyone's nerves so much that it was her own fault really but I felt bad and Greg got frightened so I tried to fetch him home. But there were people everywhere and we got threatened with a shovel by Aunty Gwladys, I don't think she knew it was me because of the monkey mask. Then someone blew up Catman's car. I am sleeping with

Greg tonight because he is still frightened. I hope I'll be able to sleep too. I don't think mam will ever let us have a Halloween party again.

Thursday 1st November 1979

Everyone was talking about last night. Raquel and Samantha had a fight. Had toad in the hole for tea.

Friday 2nd November 1979

It is Friday so me and Susan have been around the neighbours selling vegetables. Called in Aunty Ann's with mam. Laurence fell down the toilet. Exciting news, he is having a sister or brother.

Saturday 3rd November 1979

Sharon Tingle rang to say there was no piano lesson today. Went up the mountain on my bike with Susan instead. Mam is making a sheepskin rug. It is soaking in the bath.

Sunday 4th November 1979

Bod was on this morning, Greg was happy. The sheepskin is still in the bath. I don't mind but Susan isn't very pleased. She likes her baths. Listened to the top 40. Still the awful number 1.

Monday 5th November 1979

Bonfire night. We went over the pub to Dai Jones' bonfire. Axford, Peatsy and Tibbsy were there. Had fireworks. The roman candles were the best. Had crisps and got back at 9pm.

Tuesday 6th November 1979

We made breakfast in cookery class. Fruit juice, scrambled egg, toast and coffee. It was mine and Jacquelyn Butler's turn to sit at the dining table. Grange Hill was on BBC2 this evening. Mr Mitchell made Trisha walk to school with Simon, and Gary Hargreaves got jealous and threatened him. Poor Simon.

Wednesday 7th November 1979

We had to write an essay in English about the future, 1989. I wrote about Space Invaders, the new arcade game, developing brains and taking over the world. Maria's essay was the best, it was funny.

Thursday 8th November 1979

Ann has gone to Bridgewater. There is no school next Wednesday so me and Keri G are making plans to go down Ty'r Graig to see Mr Parfitt. Donna Summer, Abba, Madness and Dr Hook were on Top of the Pops. Not even going to mention Lena Martell.

Friday 9th November 1979

Mrs English is in a bad mood these days. Julie thinks she's hard as nails, she threatened me, but I'm not worried. Ann is going to call for me tomorrow. I have a sore finger.

Saturday 10th November 1979

Ann didn't call for me after all. Mam killed the cockerel. My finger is very sore. It's where I bit my nail.

Sunday 11th November 1979

My finger is even sorer. Made rock cakes. Watched the last episode of Roots. Taped the top 40. There is a new thing out called a Sony Walkman where you can listen to your tape whilst jogging and stuff.

Monday 12th November 1979

The most embarrassing day. We were made to sit in the hall and watch a film about growing up. To make things even worse, my finger has started to go green.

Tuesday 13th November 1979

Miss Biology told me I needed to go to the doctors about my green finger. Mam is cross this evening, another strip of glass has cracked on the Parkray and they are expensive. Watched Rolf Harris Cartoon Time.

Wednesday 14th November 1979

No school today. Mam took me to Dr Hussain in Six Bells about my finger. He asked if I was a cannibal and gave me penicillin. It might have to be lanced off. Me, Keri G and Ann went down Ty'r Graig to see Mr Parfitt this afternoon.

Thursday 15th November 1979

Susan went to gymnastics without me, my finger is too sore and horrid. Watched Top of the Pops. At last a new number 1. Still not brilliant though. Dr Hook, When you're in Love with a Beautiful Woman. Thin Lizzy and the Tourists were good.

Friday 16th November 1979

My finger burst in geography class. I am very glad. Mrs Geography sent me to Miss Biology to sort it. She had to tell the class to settle down. Posted a birthday card to Jackie Llewellyn. Miss Bermuda won Miss World 1979.

Saturday 17th November 1979

It is Jackie Llewellyn's birthday. Went over Grama's, she has got a new twin tub. My hair was bad today, I'm turning into Crystal Tipps with a cowlick. I wish I had nice straight hair like Claire Giles.

Sunday 18th November 1979

Mam couldn't use the phone this afternoon because Uncle Jeff had blocked the party line. He didn't put their phone down properly. Mam was shouting and whistling down the phone but they couldn't hear her, so she sent me over their house to tell them.

Monday 19th November 1979

Susan fetched the Webb Ivory catalogue home from school, had fun choosing Christmas cards to give out to my friends. There is something that I would really love for myself – the dairy milk miniatures money box. Had long division sums for maths homework. I hate them.

Tuesday 20th November 1979

Today we found out that although Mr Chemistry lives not far from Brynithel, he is very rich. His wife owns a shop in town. Watched Angels this evening.

Wednesday 21st November 1979

Poor Bulldog. The boys were playing up today, he got so angry that he slammed his hat on the floor and jumped on it. When he picked it back up, it was squashed. I think he was upset.

Thursday 22nd November 1979

Peatsy's birthday. Went to gymnastics. Mam called to see Pat. Ozzie has given us an electronic Pong game so we can play table tennis on the television.

Friday 23rd November 1979

No school for me. Went to International shopping with mam. Seen Natalie Howells' mam outside Rediffusion. Bought Blue Jeans but very disappointed that Cliff Richard was the pull-out poster. We met Laurence from Six Bells nursery and looked after him this afternoon.

Saturday 24th November 1979

Helped Dad. We had to go in the tractor through Brynithel. Mam and Dad don't understand how much people get made fun of in school. I am already being made fun of because of my hair, my skirt and my satchel. I was so worried about being seen, I asked if I could hide in the trailer. Now mam and dad think I am ridiculous. I'm not liking being anywhere at the moment.

Sunday 25th November 1979

Grama and Grandad came up for tea. Mam made salmon sandwiches. I have found a good radio station. Radio Luxembourg. Have taken the radio to bed with me. There is a stonking new song out, Walking on the Moon by the Police.

Monday 26th November 1979

Mam is getting the sheepskin nice and fluffy ready for Ty'r Graig Christmas Fayre on Friday. She is donating it as a raffle prize. Watched Ivor the Engine with Greg.

Tuesday 27th November 1979

Miss Biology made us collect leaves from the yard today. They turn brown because of a thing called tannin which is also in tea. We made tea in class. It was foul. Another good song in the charts, Brass in Pocket by the Pretenders.

Wednesday 28th November 1979

Laurence has gone to hospital. We are all worried. Pat and Ozzie have bought the Mount Pleasant pub in Brynithel. Brian and Gail got married in Coronation Street. We are doing exams in school.

Thursday 29th November 1979

Laurence is home from hospital. More exciting news, there's going to be another new baby in the family, first Baby

Brickell and now Baby Waters. A strange new song on Top of the Pops. There is no band, just a video of children being minced. Hey Teacher Leave those Kids Alone.

Friday 30th November 1979

Ty'r Graig Christmas Fayre. Mr Reed fell in love with the sheepskin and bought it for himself. Bought a bag, a dusty bin and a picture. Entered 'Guess the number of sweets' and won the whole jar. It was a dream come true.

Ty'r Graig Christmas Fayre 1979

Saturday 1st December 1979

Uncle Jeff drove straight past me when I was walking up the hill from piano lessons. I was very disappointed. He didn't recognise me because he was being absent minded. Digger Barnes is back in Dallas.

Sunday 2nd December 1979

Horrible horrible. Was doing handstands over the barn and didn't see the dog poo, it was a white one. My hand went straight in. I've been off my food all day.

Monday 3rd December 1979

My Christmas list:
- Susan – twister (£4.28 Kays catalogue)
- Greg – beano (£1.25 newsagents)
- Mam – terry towelling pyjamas (£10.79 Kays catalogue)
- Dad – liquors (£1 Woolworths)
- Aunty Ann – milk tray bar (30p Woolworths)
- Uncle Jeff – seeds (30p Woolworths)
- Laurence – blackboard and chalk (£1.55 Webb Ivory)
- Grama – picture (Christmas fayre)
- Aunty Hazel – oven gloves (that I am making in needlework)
- Aunty Sue – dusty bin (Christmas fayre)

- Aunty Lynne – bag (Christmas fayre)
- Friends and Mrs Lane – bath salts (homemade)

*Friends – Ann Davies, Jacquelyn Butler, Claire Mitchell, Keri G, Debbie Tibbs, Maria.

*Bath salts recipe (Blue Peter) – box of soda crystals (need to buy), food colouring (from cupboard), squirt perfume (mam's Tweed), clean jam jars (need to ask mam and Aunty Ann), pieces pretty material to cover lid (need to ask mam and Aunty Ann), elastic bands (will need to look around house).

Tuesday 4th December 1979

Mam went to Abergavenny market and bought the soda crystals I need to make the bath salts. Watched Animal Magic. Johnny Morris is good with animals but it's a bit far-fetched.

Wednesday 5th December 1979

We had a little handwriting competition in English class today. I won but I didn't enjoy the prize – it was to write the addresses on Mrs English's Christmas card envelopes. It took me ages and she complained that I didn't write as nicely on the envelopes as I did in the competition.

Thursday 6th December 1979

Finished paying club. It has taken 20 weeks. Someone spat on Mr Deputy's head when he was walking underneath the top wall in the yard. He went mad. The school is putting on a Christmas concert. We have to wear white school shirts and sing Little Donkey. The Christmas tree is up in the hall.

Friday 7th December 1979

Lots of exam results today. Geography 60%, History 60%, RE 80%, Science 71%, Maths 86% (shock), English 92% (biggest shock because it was a higher mark than the brainiest girl in the class). Stayed behind in school to practise the Christmas carol concert. Little Donkey didn't go too well.

Saturday 8th December 1979

Took Greg's dog Gnasher for a walk across the lane but he wouldn't come back. Started writing my Christmas cards. The Police is number 1 with Walking on the Moon.

Sunday 9th December 1979

Made the bath salts. Mixed the soda crystals with blue food colouring and squirted with perfume. Like they showed on Blue Peter. Put into jam jars and covered the lids with material held on with elastic bands. I have decided to buy Ann a writing book instead.

Monday 10th December 1979

Keri G isn't going to the school Christmas disco on Thursday. It is a shame. Eddie Kidd has done a big scary jump on his motorbike. The wind nearly blew him off. Watched Butterflies.

Tuesday 11th December 1979

Mam went to Abergavenny market and bought Greg a plastic hippo that goes in the bath, you pull the string out of his mouth and it chases a fish. Finished the oven gloves. Bunhead gave me a good mark.

Wednesday 12th December 1979

Today we saw Miss PE in a flash car. Looking forward to the Christmas disco tomorrow. Mam has sewn me a black clutch bag and I have found where I put the disco dust that came free with Blue Jeans.

Thursday 13th December 1979

School Christmas disco. Had a bath and put on my black cords, red punk shirt and disco dust. Took my clutch bag. The bus that took us there was posh, it had lights on the inside. I could do all the dances. Had 2 cans of coke and 3 packets of crisps. Mr PE and Mr History dressed up as ballerinas. Miss History and Miss Biology dressed up as Laurel and Hardy. It was good fun. Nigel Creed got into trouble, he fetched his Sex Pistols record with him and swapped Boogie Wonderland for Friggin in the Riggin.

Friday 14th December 1979

Had a go at making the Blue Peter Advent Crown out of wire hangers and tinsel this evening. It looks rubbish. Me and Greg watched Monkey on BBC2, a strange Chinese programme about Monkey who hatched out of an egg and his friends Pigsy and Sandy.

Saturday 15th December 1979

Raquel's dogs weren't there today. It was nice to walk down to piano lessons without being barked at or chased. Then went to Diane's the hairdressers. I asked for a shag but was disappointed, my hair needs to be longer I think, like Susie Quatro's. Uncle Dave and Aunty Sue came up and brought presents. We gave them theirs and one for Jackie Llewellyn.

Sunday 16th December 1979

Greg is very excited about Christmas. Made up a Christmas story for him about a robin called Robin. Something sad happened this evening. There was a mouse in the trap. We thought it was dead so mam threw it on the Parkray but it came alive and was scratching at the glass to get out. Me and Susan were crying, dad was shouting and mam was panicking. The mouse is now definitely dead.

Monday 17th December 1979

Had present off Debbie Tibbs. I think it is bubble bath. None of the boys have wrote cards or bought presents. Went down Ty'r Graig to see Susan in her Christmas play. We had a packet of Pacers on the way home.

Tuesday 18th December 1979

Made a Yule Log in cookery. It was fun. Had presents off Ann and Maria. Bubble bath off Ann and soap in the shape of a cassette tape off Maria. Met mam in Woolies after school, got the things off my list and then over to the Co-op department store. Then back to school for the concert. It went very well indeed.

Wednesday 19th December 1979

Last day of school. Took the bath salts to give out to my friends. Had bubble bath off Claire Mitchell and a green velvet diary/address book off Jacquelyn Butler. Cauline

Lewis stomped around the desks plonking bath beads in front of everyone, no wrapping paper or merry Christmas or anything, she is such a tomboy. Everyone was in a good mood today, even the teachers.

Thursday 20th December 1979

First day of Christmas holidays. Went with mam to Leo's in Pontllanfraith then to Grama's. Me and Susan are staying here tonight. Mam bought lots of goodies in Leo's. Can't wait to go back home and start eating them. We made paperchains and helped Grama put them up.

Friday 21st December 1979

Grandad drove me and Susan to Aunty Hazel's. We are staying here tonight. Had a lovely dinner then went to Blackwood in a car. Had a bath in Aunty Hazel's house. It is nice and warm here, I like it. Had coffee cheesecake.

Saturday 22nd December 1979

Susan was playing with Uncle Kevin this morning. I felt left out. I tried playing with Silky the cat but she bit me. Came back home this afternoon. Our tree is up. It looks lovely. Mam has decorated it with Quality Streets. I made icing for the Christmas cake. Greg is ill.

Sunday 23rd December 1979

Greg is worse. Went over Aunty Ann's with my presents. Uncle Jeff was in a bad mood. Laurence has had a letter off Father Christmas. It was snowing. Susan went down Brynithel to give presents to Natalie and Samantha but came back crying because of Raquel's dogs. I feel sorry for Nigel Creed, it is his birthday today but no one is caring about birthdays because they are too busy thinking about Christmas. Mam thinks a mouse has been at the sweets on the tree. Ha.

Monday 24th December 1979

Mam called the doctor to see Greg. He came at 4.30pm. Greg has to stay in bed for 10 days. He has the measles. Me and Susan made foil cone baubles for the tree and watched It's a Christmas Knockout and the Val Doonigan Christmas Show. Very excited now.

Tuesday 25th December 1979

Christmas Day. We had metal roller skates with straps to tie up over our shoes. Me and Susan skated over to Aunty Ann's. Laurence had a Fisher Price garage. Grama and Grandad came up for dinner. Susan and Greg had guitars. Susan's is very quiet, Grama accidentally bought an electric one, she didn't realise it needed an amplifier. They gave Laurence £1. Watched Christmas Top of the Tops. Blondie, Boney M, Dr Hook, Gary Numan, the Police, BA Robertson, Roxy Music. Pink Floyd Brick in the Wall is the Christmas number 1. Susan made me marzipan fruits, my favourite thing. Played Twister. Watched the Mike Yarwood Christmas Show on BBC then Christmas with Eric and Ernie on HTV. Had a really nice day.

Tuesday 26th December 1979

Boxing Day. Went over Grama's with dad and Susan. Mam had to stay home with Greg and his measles. Had nice time with Uncle Dave and Aunty Sue. They liked their bin. Grama put her picture up and Aunty Hazel was very pleased with her oven gloves. Grama opened her Mackintosh Weekend chocolates. Mam and dad went over Aunty Ann's this evening. Me and Susan watched Man about the House.

Thursday 27th December 1979

Keri G's birthday but no one is in school to say happy birthday. Mam, Aunty Betty, Aunty Lynne, Aunty Hazel and Uncle Dave are clubbing together to buy Grama and Grandad a colour TV for their 40th anniversary. It is a surprise. Susan's roller skate broke. Aberbeeg is flooded.

Friday 28th December 1979

Dad went to Abertillery to pick up the papers. Farmers Weekly for him, Blue Jeans for me, Bunty for Susan, Beano for Greg. Maria rang up to see if I wanted to see Tom Thumb in the pictures. Everything was free. It was good. There is a new film being advertised called Mad Max which looks cool. Loads of people are getting Betamax and VHS recorders. They are arguing about which one is best.

Saturday 29th December 1979

Mam walked me past Raquel's dogs so I could get to piano lessons. Peter Hatton was knocking on Raquel's door. Me and Susan babysat for Aunty Ann and Uncle Jeff. They have a portable TV which means they can watch telly in the kitchen. It is amazing. Had good game with Laurence and his Fisher Price garage. Watched Dallas. Aunty Ann and Uncle Jeff got back at 9.55pm with chips. We had chip butties and slept there.

Sunday 30th December 1979

Susan found £2. It was Uncle Jeff's, he gave her 20p for finding it. Aunty Ann walked us home at 10.30am. Dilwyn was spying on us. Susan tried wearing Greg's roller skates as hers are broke but she nearly broke her leg too so she went back inside. Taped the top 40. Pink Floyd Another Brick in the Wall is number 1 in the singles chart and Rod Stewart Greatest Hits is number 1 in the album charts.

Monday 31st December 1979 /
Tuesday 1st January 1980

Mam and dad went down to the Mount Pleasant Inn for New Year's Eve and didn't get back until 1.30am. Susan and I stayed up late watching the Kenny Everett Show. Aunty Lynne came to visit with Grama. Dad got into trouble. He thought they had gone so let off a big bit of wind but they came back in. No-one could breathe and Aunty Lynne's eyes were watering as she struggled with the door latch to get back out. Quarrelled with Susan, she is a fat thing. This is the end of my 1979 diary.

Thank you to everyone named in the diary and to the families of those named but sadly no longer with us. You have all been such good sports and have made this publication possible. A special thank you to Keri Gould who put tremendous efforts into tracking down people and getting their permissions, to John Hancock for the photographs of Ty'r Graig school, to Martin Hearson for the photographs of Henleys buses, to PetersensPR and their client Tillery Valley Foods for the photograph overlooking Abertillery, to Alamy for the photograph of Six Bells Colliery, to TVFilmProps for the photographs of 1979 items and to Megan-Sian Photography for assistance with getting photographs print ready. Elizabeth Baker-Bartlett wishes to thank Bakehouse Print Limited, Kevin, Emily and Sam for their help with illustrations.